HUMAN BODY

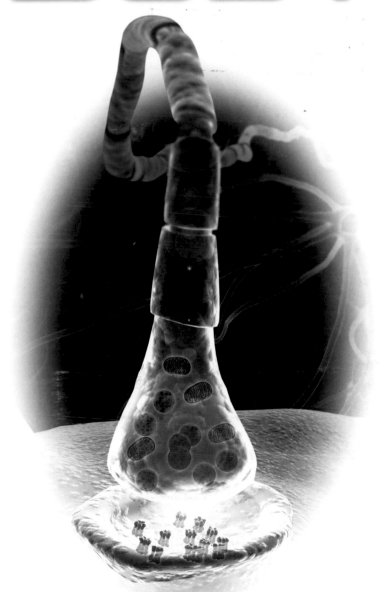

Miranda Smith

KINGFISHER
NEW YORK

KINGFISHER
LONDON & NEW YORK

Copyright © 2008 by Kingfisher
Published in the United States by Kingfisher
175 Fifth Ave., New York, NY 10010
Kingfisher is an imprint of Macmillan Children's Books, London.
All rights reserved.

Distributed in the U.S. by Macmillan, 175 Fifth Ave., New York, NY 10010

Consultant: Dr. Patricia Macnair
3-D body illustrations: Rajeev Doshi at Medi-Mation

First published in 2008 by Kingfisher
First published in paperback in 2011 by Kingfisher

LIBRARY OF CONGRESS CATALOGING-IN-PUBLICATION DATA
Smith, Miranda.
Navigators. Human body / Miranda Smith.—1st American ed.
p. cm.
Includes index.
1. Human anatomy—Juvenile literature. 2. Human physiology—Juvenile literature. I. Title. II. Title: Human body.
QM27.S65 2008
612—dc22

2007047764

ISBN: 978-0-7534-6683-4

Kingfisher books are available for special promotions and premiums. For details contact:
Special Markets Department, Macmillan, 175 Fifth Avenue, New York NY 10010.

Printed in China
1 3 5 7 9 8 6 4 2

1TR/0411/WKT/UNTD/140MA

Note to readers: The website addresses listed in this book are correct at the time of publishing.
However, due to the ever-changing nature of the Internet, website addresses and content can change.
Websites can contain links that are unsuitable for children. The publisher cannot be held responsible
for changes in website addresses or content or for information obtained through third-party websites.
We strongly advise that Internet searches are supervised by an adult.

The Publisher would like to thank the following for permission to reproduce their images (t = top, b = bottom, c = center, l = left, r = right):
Page 1 Getty/3D4Medical.com; 3tl Science Photo Library (SPL)/NIAID/CDC; 3bc SPL/Biology Media; 5tl Getty/Stone; 5tr SPL/Living Art Enterprises, LLC;
6cr SPL/Robert Brocksmith; 6bl SPL/ISM; 7t SPL/Professor P. Motta/Dept. of Anatomy/La Sapienza, Rome, Italy; 7cl SPL/Andrew Syred; 7bl Getty/Visuals
Unlimited; 7cr SPL/Steve Gschmeissner; 7br SPL/Steve Gschmeissner; 8cl SPL/David Parker; 8cr SPL/James King-Holmes; 8bl SPL/Andrew Syred;
8–9 SPL/Pasieka; 9tl SPL/J. C. Revy; 9tr SPL/J. L. Carson, Custom Medical Stock Photo; 9br SPL/Pasieka; 10–11 Corbis/Randy Faris; 10br SPL/Alfred Pasieka;
11ct SPL/Steve Gschmeissner; 11cr SPL/Andrew Syred; 11cb Shutterstock; 12br SPL/BSIP, Chassenet; 13cr Getty/Visuals Unlimited; 13bl Corbis/Carl &
Ann Purcell; 13br SPL/Eye of Science; 14tr Shutterstock; 14bl SPL/Steve Gschmeissner; 14br Shutterstock; 14–15 Corbis/Kai Pfaffenbach/Reuters;
15ct Shutterstock; 15c Shutterstock; 15cl SPL/D Roberts; 15bl Shutterstock; 15br Shutterstock; 16cl SPL/Steve Gschmeissner; 16cr Getty/3D4medical.com;
16bc Getty/Taxi; 17tr SPL/Alfred Pasieka; 17bc SPL/Manfred Kage; 17br SPL/Andrew Syred; 18tl SPL/Eye of Science; 18cl SPL/Susumu Nishinaga;
19tr SPL/Steve Gschmeissner; 20tr SPL/AJ Photo; 20c SPL/John Bavosi; 20bl SPL/NIAID/CDC; 20br SPL/Steve Gschmeissner; 21 SPL/Thierry Berrod,
Mona Lisa Production; 21b SPL/Biology Media; 22 SPL; 22br SPL/Asa Thoresen; 23tr SPL; 23cr SPL/L. Steinmark/Custom Medical Stock Photo; 23b SPL;
24br SPL/Susumu Nishinaga; 25tl Corbis/Pete Saloutos; 25tr Getty/Visuals Unlimited; 25cl Corbis/Visuals Unlimited; 25bl SPL/John Bavosi; 25br Corbis/
Ned Frisk; 26 Getty/3D4Medical.com; 26r Getty/AFP; 27 Getty/3D4Medical.com; 27tr Getty/Visuals Unlimited; 27br SPL/Eye of Science; 28bl SPL/
Mehau Kulyk; 29c SPL/James Holmes; 29b Getty/Science Faction; 30cl Corbis/Darama; 30br Getty/Taxi; 31cl SPL/Eye of Science; 31bl SPL/Professor
Cinti & V. Gremet; 32tl SPL/David Parker; 32bl Getty/Stockbyte; 33tr SPL/Steve Percival; 33c SPL/Omikron; 33br Corbis/Gary W. Carter; 34bl SPL/Steve
Gschmeissner; 34cr Getty/Collection Mix; 35c SPL/Roger Harris; 35cr SPL/Alfred Pasieka; 35b Getty/Jamie Harnwell; 36tc Getty/Photonica; 36tr SPL/
Alex Bartel; 36bl SPL/Eye of Science; 37tc SPL/Eye of Science; 37tr SPL/Steve Gschmeissner; 38 Getty/Visuals Unlimited; 38c Getty/Collection Mix;
38cr SPL/Steve Gschmeissner; 38br SPL/CNRI; 39t SPL/Alain Pol, ISM; 39cr SPL/Alfred Pasieka; 39b SPL; 40 SPL/Steve Gschmeissner; 40r SPL/Roger
Harris; 41l SPL/Roger Harris; 41bl SPL/Du Cane Medical Imaging Ltd.; 41br SPL/Sovereign, ISM; 42tr SPL/Eye of Science; 43 Getty/3D4Medical.com;
43br Getty/Stone+; 44l SPL/Professor P. Motta/Dept. of Anatomy/La Sapienza, Rome, Italy; 44c SPL/Susumu Nishinaga; 44r SPL/ISM; 45l SPL/NIAID/CDC;
45c SPL/Pasieka; 45r Getty/3D4Medical.com; 48tr Photolibrary.com; 48cl Corbis/Neal Preston; 48br Corbis/Bettman Archive

CONTENTS

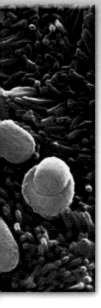

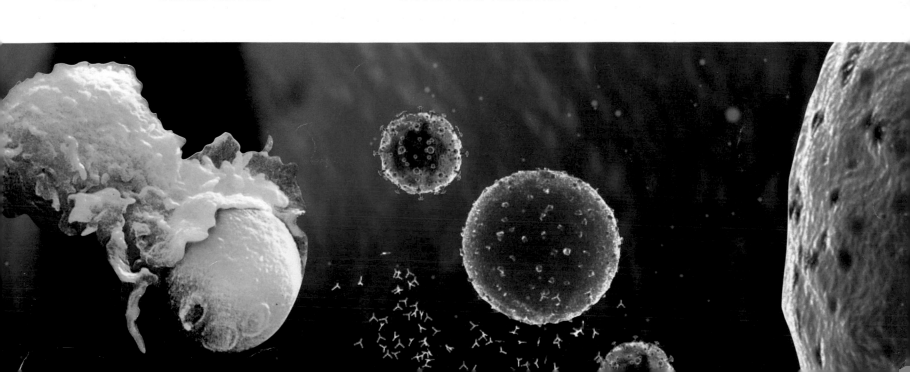

SYSTEMS IN UNISON

The human body is an extraordinary machine with several intricate parts that all help keep the body working. At the heart of this machine there are ten internal body systems that interact to make everything run smoothly. Each system has an individual and vital role, and together they maintain the body's health and efficiency. Covering the entire body is another system, the integumentary system—the skin, hair, and nails that contain and protect the rest.

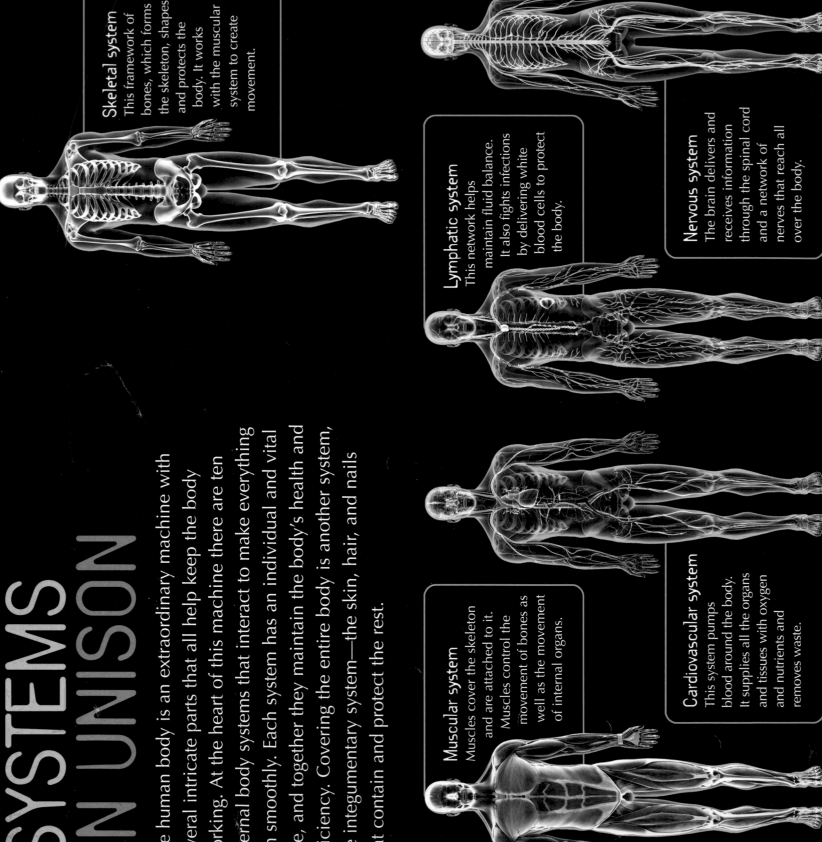

Skeletal system
This framework of bones, which forms the skeleton, shapes and protects the body. It works with the muscular system to create movement.

Lymphatic system
This network helps maintain fluid balance. It also fights infections by delivering white blood cells to protect the body.

Nervous system
The brain delivers and receives information through the spinal cord and a network of nerves that reach all over the body.

Muscular system
Muscles cover the skeleton and are attached to it. Muscles control the movement of bones as well as the movement of internal organs.

Cardiovascular system
This system pumps blood around the body. It supplies all the organs and tissues with oxygen and nutrients and removes waste.

> **SYSTEM**—a group of organs and tissues that are associated with a particular bodily function

● BODY IMAGING

Today, techniques have been developed to look inside the human body. Since the invention of x-rays, doctors have been able to see the body's internal workings without having to cut someone open. Computerized axial tomography (CAT), magnetic resonance imaging (MRI), and ultrasound scans have all led to greater accuracy in the diagnosis and treatment of illnesses.

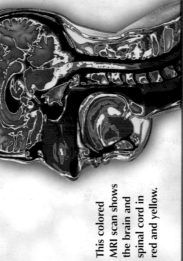

This colored MRI scan shows the brain and spinal cord in red and yellow.

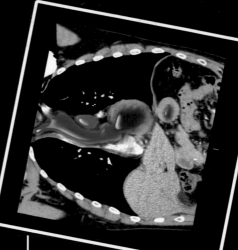

Body organs

Different organs are at the center of each of the body's systems—for example, the heart in the cardiovascular system and the brain in the nervous system. In some systems, several organs are linked to fulfill a particular task. In the digestive system, the stomach, intestines, and liver process food and absorb nutrients.

This colored CAT scan shows the heart (blue, center) and the liver (green, bottom left).

Endocrine system
Glands and cells produce chemical messengers called hormones that help control body processes such as reproduction and growth.

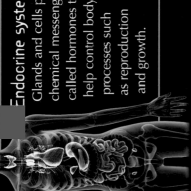

Urinary system
The kidneys make urine and process waste, maintaining a good balance of fluids, minerals, and salts in the body.

Respiratory system
Breathing muscles push air into and out of the lungs. The lungs absorb the oxygen from the air into the blood. Oxygen is needed by the body's tissues.

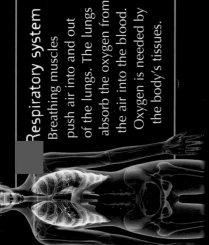

Digestive system
This system runs from the mouth to the anus, processing food, absorbing nutrients, and getting rid of waste.

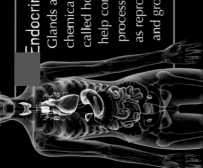

Reproductive systems
The male reproductive organs produce sperm. The female reproductive organs produce ripe eggs. The female body also carries and nourishes a baby until it is ready to be born.

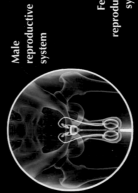

Male reproductive system

Female reproductive system

> The central nervous system is connected to every single part of the body.

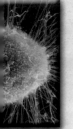

ESSENTIAL CELLS

We are all made up of cells, which are often described as the "building blocks of life." All human cells are tiny—too small to be seen, except through a microscope. They multiply as people grow, so a ten-year-old child will have only around half the number of cells that his or her parents have. Cells are highly organized. They process the food that is absorbed by the body, turning it into energy so that the cells can carry out different activities.

Endoplasmic reticulum transports materials through the cell.

nucleus

Gogli body processes proteins.

protective cell membrane

mitochondrion

cytoplasm

Cell division by mitosis: a single cell produces two identical daughter cells

The cell's power plants

Mitochondria are organelles ("little organs") found in a cell that are made up of water and proteins called enzymes. The enzymes take in nutrients, break them down, and combine the sugar glucose with oxygen. This chemical process, called cellular respiration, releases energy for the cell to use.

Cell structure

At the center of most body cells is a nucleus that contains DNA (see pages 8–9). The nucleus also controls cell division and reproduction. It is surrounded by jellylike cytoplasm in which mitochondria float. The mitochondria give the cell energy, while the cytoplasm transforms that energy for use by the body. A membrane surrounds the cell, controlling what enters and leaves.

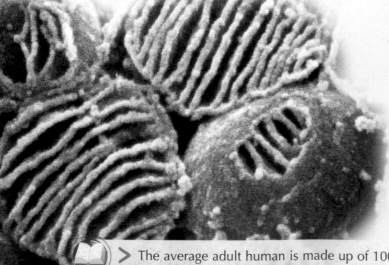

Cell division

There are two types of cell division. Mitosis (right) happens when the body needs more cells, either for growth or to repair damage. A "parent cell" produces two exact copies of itself, known as "daughter cells," in a process called replication. The other type of cell division is called meiosis and produces gametes, or sex cells, for reproduction (see pages 42–43).

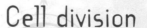

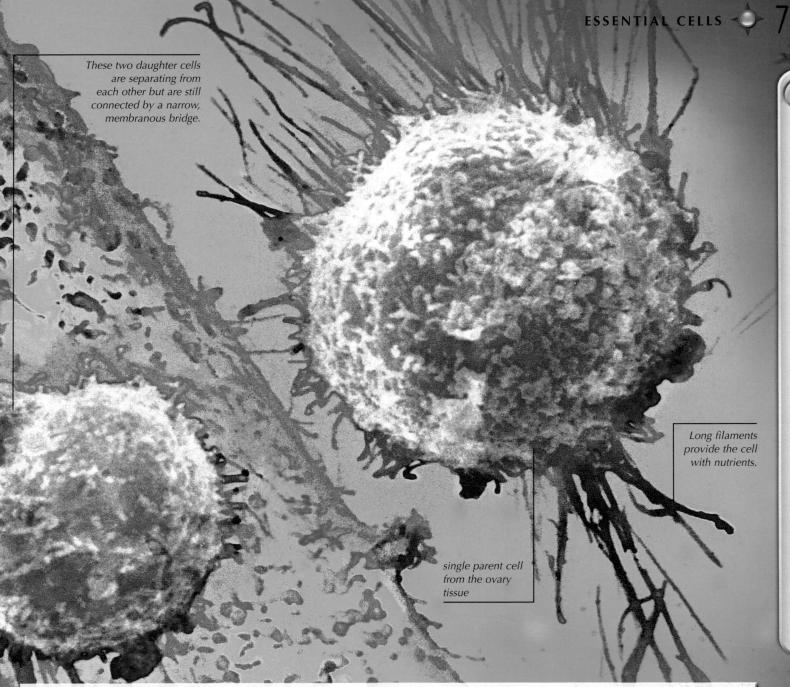

These two daughter cells are separating from each other but are still connected by a narrow, membranous bridge.

Long filaments provide the cell with nutrients.

single parent cell from the ovary tissue

http://science.howstuffworks.com/environmental/life/cellular-microscopic/cell.htm

⊖ TYPES OF CELLS

There are around 200 different types of cells. Cells are usually arranged into tissues, which themselves contain many cells that perform the same function. For example, liver cells work together to remove toxic chemicals from the blood.

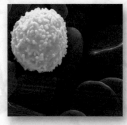

White blood cells produce antibodies and fight diseases.
Red blood cells absorb and release oxygen.

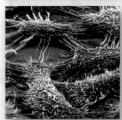

Epithelial cells form the upper layer of the skin, as well as protecting the body's blood vessels and intestines.

This is an osteocyte, a type of **bone cell** that maintains the structure that gives bones their strength and hardness.

Neurons (nerve cells) generate and conduct electrical impulses that communicate between the nervous system and the rest of the body.

GENES AND DNA

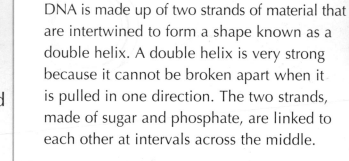

"The information encoded in your DNA determines your unique biological characteristics such as sex, eye color, age, and Social Security number."

Dave Barry (born 1947)
American writer and comedian

Genes carry the instructions for making your body. Every person's genes are unique, except in the case of identical twins. You get half of your genes from your mother and half from your father. Identical sets of genes are stored in the nucleus of all body cells. Inside of each nucleus, a chemical called DNA forms long strands, which are called chromosomes. A gene is one section of a chromosome.

The DNA double helix

DNA is made up of two strands of material that are intertwined to form a shape known as a double helix. A double helix is very strong because it cannot be broken apart when it is pulled in one direction. The two strands, made of sugar and phosphate, are linked to each other at intervals across the middle.

computer display of a human DNA sequence

Genes and mapping

In 2001, scientists made a map of the genes that are necessary to build a person. They did this by tracing a complete DNA sequence for the human body. This set of genes, called the human genome, is vital to the development of medicines.

a researcher preparing DNA for sequencing

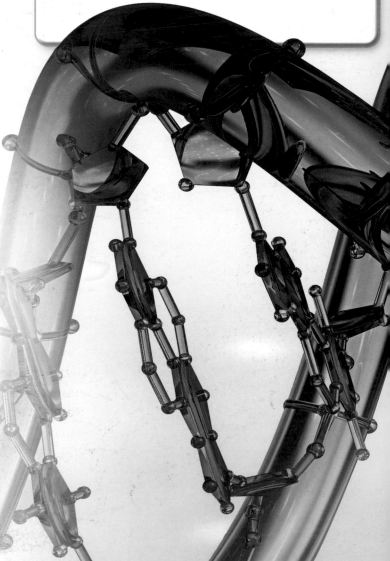

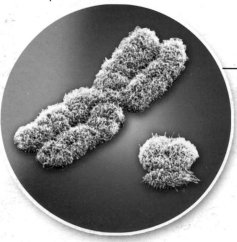

Chromosomes

Each cell nucleus contains 46 chromosomes in 23 pairs. One of these pairs are sex chromosomes, called X and Y chromosomes because of their shape. These are responsible for deciding what sex a person is. Males have one X and one Y chromosome, while females have two X chromosomes.

 > Humans share 98.4 percent of their DNA with chimpanzees and 70 percent with slugs.

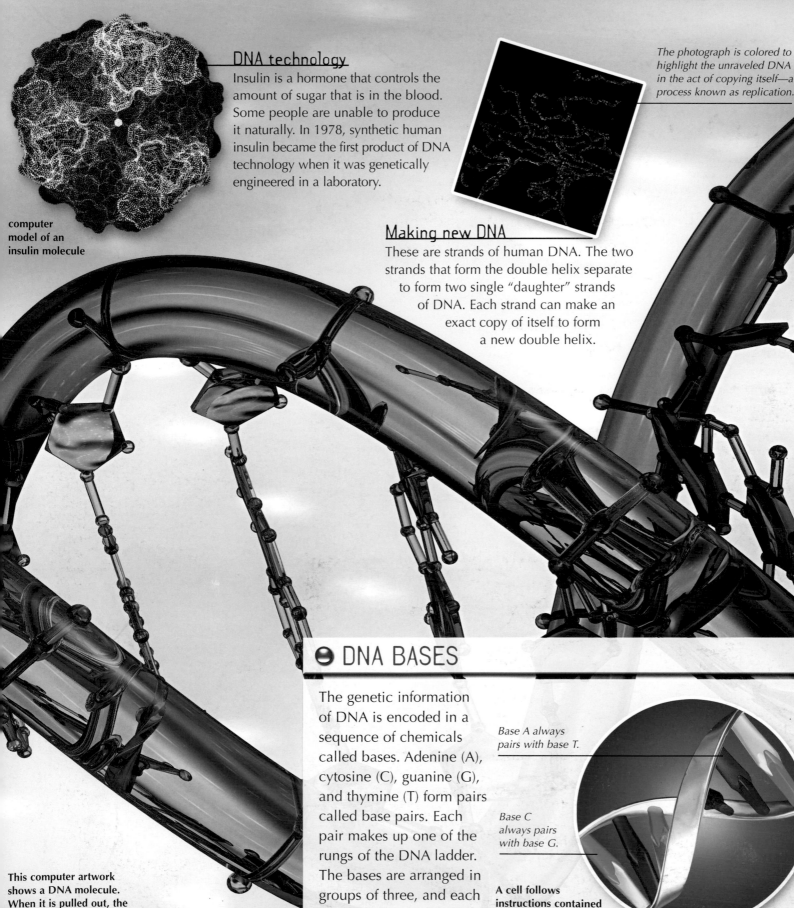

DNA technology

Insulin is a hormone that controls the amount of sugar that is in the blood. Some people are unable to produce it naturally. In 1978, synthetic human insulin became the first product of DNA technology when it was genetically engineered in a laboratory.

computer model of an insulin molecule

The photograph is colored to highlight the unraveled DNA in the act of copying itself—a process known as replication.

Making new DNA

These are strands of human DNA. The two strands that form the double helix separate to form two single "daughter" strands of DNA. Each strand can make an exact copy of itself to form a new double helix.

www.sciencemuseum.org.uk/WhoAmI/FindOutMore/Yourgenes.aspx

⊖ DNA BASES

The genetic information of DNA is encoded in a sequence of chemicals called bases. Adenine (A), cytosine (C), guanine (G), and thymine (T) form pairs called base pairs. Each pair makes up one of the rungs of the DNA ladder. The bases are arranged in groups of three, and each group works as a code.

Base A always pairs with base T.

Base C always pairs with base G.

A cell follows instructions contained in the way that the groups of bases are arranged.

This computer artwork shows a DNA molecule. When it is pulled out, the DNA double helix looks like a twisted ladder.

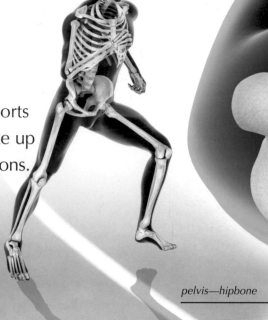

SKELETON

The strong, articulated framework of the skeleton supports and shapes the rest of the body. The 206 bones that make up the average skeleton vary in size and have different functions. Long bones, such as those found in the arms and legs, act as levers to change the position of the limbs. Flat bones in the skull and ribs, and irregular bones such as the vertebrae in the spine, protect the organs.

pelvis—hipbone

Bone structure

In the center of a long bone is a cavity that carries bone marrow. Around the marrow is a layer of spongy bone. A thin membrane, the periosteum, covers the hard outer layer of compact bone. All bones contain blood vessels, nerve cells, and living bone cells called osteocytes, osteoblasts, and osteoclasts. These make the bone, maintain it, and store minerals until they are needed.

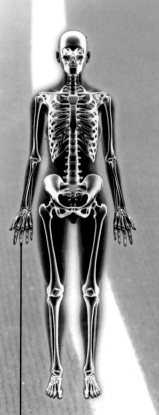

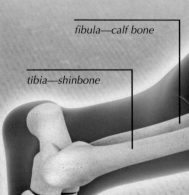

fibula—calf bone

tibia—shinbone

Skeletal system

Without a skeleton, the human body would have no shape or form. It would not be able to move, and its vital organs would have no protection. The skeletal system and muscular system work together to make the body move.

The skull

There are 22 bones in the skull. Eight of these bones form the cranium, protecting the brain and forming the forehead. The other 14 bones make up the framework for the face, including the nasal cavity and eye sockets. The only movable skull bone is the lower jaw.

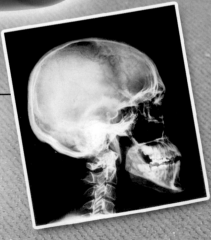

 > A newborn baby has 350 bones, but a fully grown adult has only 206. More than half of these bones are in the hands and feet.

femur—thighbone

Spongy bone

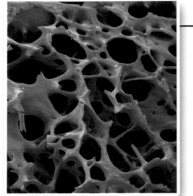

Cancellous, or spongy, bone forms the center of a bone. It is a lightweight honeycomb of spikes of bone called trabeculae, which are only a few cells thick. The spaces between the trabeculae are filled with marrow, which contains blood cells.

Bone marrow in long bones changes color from red in children to yellow in adults.

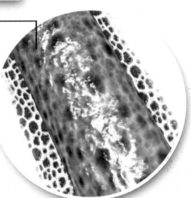

Periosteum membrane contains blood vessels that keep the bone alive.

Bone marrow stores fat and produces red blood cells.

rod-shaped osteons made up of layers of tissue called lamellae

central canal containing blood vessels and nerves

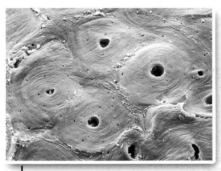

Compact bone

Cortical, or compact, bone forms an outer layer that withstands everyday stresses. It is one of the strongest materials in the human body. Its rod-shaped columns of bone, called osteons, are less than 0.04 in. (1mm) across.

⊖ GROWTH AND REPAIR

Bones can repair themselves when they are damaged. In a simple fracture such as this one, the surrounding tissues bleed, creating a clot between the broken pieces. New fibrous tissue then builds to bridge the gap between the two pieces of bone and osteoblasts multiply, forming fresh bone tissue.

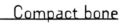

fracture to radius bone in the arm

▽ MUSCLE—*a tissue that contracts in order to move part of the body*

MUSCLES

Muscles turn the fuel in your body into energy and heat, keeping you upright and preventing your joints from dislocating. They keep your heart beating, your stomach working, and your body moving. All muscles respond to the signals that are sent through the nervous system by the brain, and they use energy to contract, or get shorter, in order to pull a particular part of the body into position.

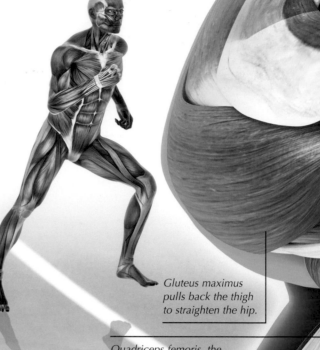

Gluteus maximus pulls back the thigh to straighten the hip.

Quadriceps femoris, the main thigh muscle, flexes and straightens the knee.

Muscles in action

When you run, the skeletal muscles in your legs work together to lift each leg, one after the other, straightening and bending the knees and adjusting the position of the feet. All muscles contract and pull; they cannot push. Muscles are arranged in pairs that work in opposition to one another. When one of a pair contracts, the opposing muscle relaxes, and vice versa.

Gastrocnemius, the main calf muscle, flexes the foot downward.

Muscular system

Every movement of the human body is created by the muscles that make up the muscular system. There are three types of muscles: skeletal, smooth, and cardiac. They cover the body in layers, and most of them are skeletal muscles.

Moving muscles

When you want to flex the muscles in your arm, your brain makes a decision to move the limb. It then sends a signal via nerve impulses, which travel along nerves to tell the biceps muscle to contract. This flexes the forearm at the elbow and turns the palm upward.

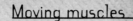

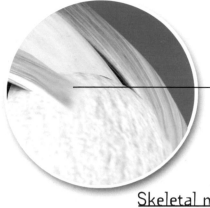

tough tendon connecting the muscle to the patella, or kneecap

Skeletal muscle

Skeletal muscles are very long and made up of bundles of fibers called myofibrils. These muscles are attached to the skeleton or to each other by tough, flexible tendons.

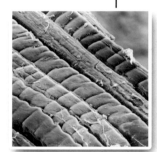

Skeletal muscles are "voluntary"—they function because you consciously make them work.

Tibialis anterior flexes the foot upward and inward.

Smooth muscle

Smooth muscle cells are small compared to skeletal muscle cells. These muscles are found in the walls of the digestive system, the bladder, the eye, the airways, and the uterus (in females).

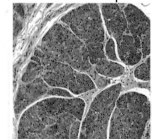

http://kidshealth.org/kid/htbw/muscles.html

Rodlike myofibrils run along the length of each skeletal muscle.

Peroneus longus flexes the foot downward and outward.

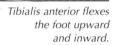

⊖ FACIAL MUSCLES

The muscles in your face do not connect to the bones. Instead, they are attached to other muscles or to the skin. This means that even the smallest contraction will change your expression. Many different muscles contribute to creating a smile. These include the four zygomaticus major and minor muscles, which pull up the corners of the mouth, and the two orbicularis oculi muscles, which encircle each eye and cause crinkling.

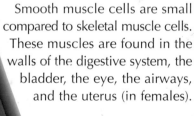

LIGAMENTS—*tough strips of connective tissue that hold bones together at a joint*

JOINTS AND LIGAMENTS

Muscles would not be able to move the skeleton unless there were articulations, or mobile joints, between the bones. Some joints move very little or not at all. However, most joints are synovial, or free moving. Bands of strong tissue called ligaments support the joints, binding the bones together.

hinge joint—the convex surface of one bone fits into the concave surface of another

Joints and movement

There are six types of synovial joints, and they each have a different range of movements. The largest of all is the knee, which is a hinge joint. One of the most mobile—allowing movement in all directions—is the shoulder, which is a ball-and-socket joint. In every synovial joint, cartilage covers and protects the ends of the bones, and synovial fluid lubricates them.

Ligaments

These are tough, fibrous cords that link bones together at a joint. They are not elastic, but they are flexible. They protect and stabilize joints by limiting their movement to certain directions. This is a magnified view of the sturdy fibers (pink) that make up a ligament.

plane, or gliding, joint—both bones are flattened and slide over each other

> We are 0.4 in. (1cm) shorter at night because our joints compress during the day.

ball-and-socket joint—the rounded head of one bone fits into the cuplike end of another

pivot joint—a protrusion from the end of one bone pivots in the ring-shaped socket of another

"The moral arc of the universe bends at the elbow of justice."

Martin Luther King, Jr. (1929–1968)
U.S. civil rights leader, speaking in Atlanta, Georgia, on August 16, 1967

⊖ THE SPINE

The joints in the spine (backbone) are called facet joints. They are hingelike and link the 33 stacked vertebrae of the spinal column. Each vertebra has two sets of facet joints— one pair facing up and the other pair facing down. The joints help make the spine flexible, but they also control any movement, protecting against a lot of pressure— for example, as the result of an accident.

http://insideout.rigb.org/insideout/anatomy/casing_the_joint/joints_explorer.html

saddle joint—each bone has both concave and convex areas, so the bones can slide back and forth and rotate

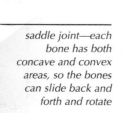

ellipsoid joint—the egg-shaped end of one bone fits into a cavity on another

∨

EPIDERMIS—*the outer layer of skin from which dead cells are worn away*

SKIN, HAIR, AND NAILS

The human body is covered with the most extraordinary of all its systems—the integumentary system. This includes your skin, hair, and nails. Your skin, the largest body organ, protects you against infections and damage. Hairs on the surface of the skin help control body temperature along with sweat glands in the skin, which enable you to perspire and cool down. Nails cover the sensitive tips of your fingers and toes, protecting them from injuries.

Hair on the head preserves heat, as well as cushioning against impact.

Hair shafts are formed from dead cells and a hard protein called keratin.

Body protection

Your skin has three main layers. The outer, waterproof epidermis is made up of layers of cells that wear away and are renewed. The dermis contains touch receptors and sebaceous glands that produce oily sebum. The subcutaneous tissue contains sweat glands and fat-storing cells, helping protect the body from damage and holding in body heat.

Hairs grow from roots, or hair bulbs, embedded in the skin.

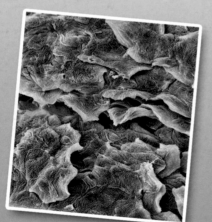

Cells in the epidermis are completely replaced every 28 days.

Hair shafts project above the skin's surface.

basal epidermis—layer where cell division supplies epidermis with new cells

Glands in the subcutaneous tissue produce sweat, which travels to the surface as perspiration.

Sebaceous glands in the hair follicles lubricate (oil) the hair and skin.

Skin surface

These cells on the surface of the epidermis are ready to flake off, while new cells move up from the basal epidermis to take their place. This outer layer of cells, the stratum corneum, is made up of dead cells.

Skin color

The color of skin depends on how much melanin it contains. Melanin coloration is decided by the genetics of the person (see pages 8–9) and by how much the skin is exposed to the sun.

 > An average person loses more than 17 oz. (500g) of skin every year.

These touch receptors in the dermis (blue) respond to pressure and vibrations.

epidermis (red)

⊖ FINGERPRINTS

At the end of our fingers are swirls of skin ridges that produce a pattern that is unique to each individual person. They leave sweat patterns called fingerprints on anything that they touch. On September 13, 1902, an English burglar named Harry Jackson became the first person to be convicted of a crime because of fingerprint evidence.

fingernail formed from the protein keratin

cuticle

nail root

matrix

bone

fat

www.bbc.co.uk/science/humanbody/body/factfiles/skin/skin.shtml

Nail structure

Fingernails and toenails are hard plates that protect sensitive skin. As the nails grow, the cells below the nail root move up toward the surface of the skin, pressing tightly together. The cells pile up in layers of keratin, which make up the nail.

BLOOD VESSELS

"The blood is the life, Mr. Renfield."

Count Dracula
from Bram Stoker's novel Dracula, 1897

In adults, 1.3–1.6 gal. (5–6L) of blood flows continuously through the body in tubes called blood vessels. Arteries carry blood from the heart to the tissues, lungs, and other organs, where it is needed. The arteries narrow into arterioles, which narrow even further into capillaries. From the tiny capillaries, deoxygenated blood travels through venules, which widen to become veins. The veins return the blood to the heart, and the process is repeated.

Plasma is the fluid that makes up 50 percent of blood.

Red blood cells carry oxygen and give blood its color.

The capillary network

Capillary walls are made up of only one layer of cells—the endothelium. This is so thin that molecules of oxygen and nutrients can pass through to be absorbed by the cells that make up body tissues. Waste products pass back into the blood to be carried away.

Cardiovascular system

This system consists of the heart, the blood vessels, and the blood itself. It circulates the blood, delivering nutrients and oxygen through arteries (red) and removing waste products through veins (blue).

Inside a blood vessel

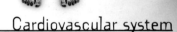

Muscular arteries have thicker walls than veins because they need to be able to control the incredible pressure of each heartbeat. The walls are made up of different layers, and the liquid blood that travels through them is made up of plasma, which carries trillions of red blood cells, white blood cells, and platelets.

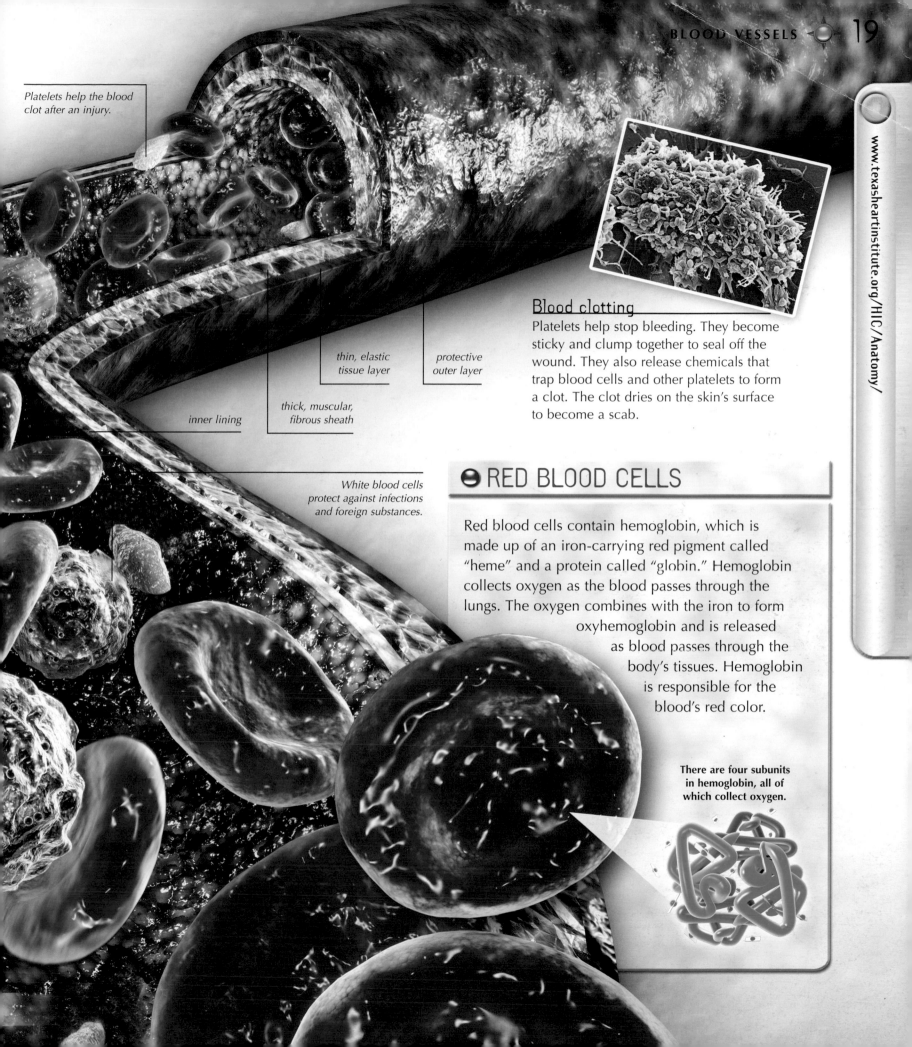

Platelets help the blood clot after an injury.

inner lining

thick, muscular, fibrous sheath

thin, elastic tissue layer

protective outer layer

White blood cells protect against infections and foreign substances.

Blood clotting

Platelets help stop bleeding. They become sticky and clump together to seal off the wound. They also release chemicals that trap blood cells and other platelets to form a clot. The clot dries on the skin's surface to become a scab.

⊖ RED BLOOD CELLS

Red blood cells contain hemoglobin, which is made up of an iron-carrying red pigment called "heme" and a protein called "globin." Hemoglobin collects oxygen as the blood passes through the lungs. The oxygen combines with the iron to form oxyhemoglobin and is released as blood passes through the body's tissues. Hemoglobin is responsible for the blood's red color.

There are four subunits in hemoglobin, all of which collect oxygen.

www.texasheartinstitute.org/HIC/Anatomy/

IMMUNITY

The human body is under attack all the time. It needs to protect itself against invaders such as bacteria, viruses, fungi, and other parasites. The skin forms an external defensive layer, and the body has cells and organisms that actively defend it. As a major part of this defensive response, a clear fluid called lymph plays a vital role by carrying immune cells throughout the body. Any invasion that gets through these defenses will lead to an infection.

⊝ IMMUNIZATION

Immunization helps the body recognize and fight a particular infection. The injection of a vaccine (above) stimulates the immune system to produce molecules called antibodies. These will then be ready to destroy the infectious microorganisms, known as pathogens, when they invade.

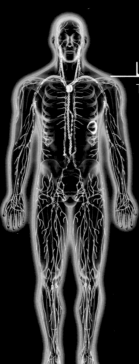

Lymphatic system

This includes vessels, nodes, the tonsils, the spleen, and the thymus gland—plus the lymph fluid, which includes white blood cells. White blood cells are the body's most powerful defense. They include macrophages and lymphocytes.

lymphocyte

Lymphocytes multiply in germinal centers.

tough, outer capsule

Valve prevents any backflow of lymph.

Lymph nodes

These small swellings are found all along the lymph vessels. They produce and store lymphocytes, which are divided into B cells and T cells. B cells produce antibodies that remember antigens (foreign substances) and attach to them. T cells destroy cells that are targeted by the B cells.

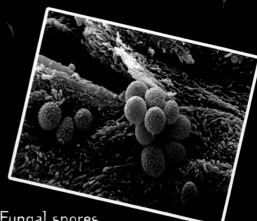

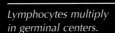

colored image of *E. coli* bacteria (blue-green)

Bacterial infection

Many bacteria live in human intestines without doing harm. One of these is *E. coli* (left). However, there are some strains of *E. coli* that are dangerous because they produce a toxin that causes diarrhea and even death.

Fungal spores

Although some fungi are useful to humans, others cause diseases and pain. One common problem is athlete's foot, in which a fungus feeds on the skin. These athlete's foot fungal spores (above) have infected a toenail.

antibodies

B lymphocytes at work

Four viruses (left) are surrounded by tiny, Y-shaped antibodies. The antibodies, also known as immunoglobulins, are proteins that are produced by B cells, and they help the immune system identify the viruses. They will either destroy these viruses themselves or tag them so that the white blood cell (right) can do it.

www.acm.uiuc.edu/sigbio/project/updated-lymphatic/lymph1.html

white blood cell

virus

"Freedom is the most contagious virus known to man."

Hubert H. Humphrey (1911–1978)

38th U.S. vice president (1965–1969)

Phagocytes

Phagocytes are cells that absorb and digest debris and invaders. They attack these invaders with enzymes, which break them down. Macrophages, and some lymphocytes, can act as phagocytes. Here, a lymphocyte (blue) begins to engulf an invading cell (yellow). It will eventually swallow and digest the intruder completely.

HEART

"The heart of the fool is in his mouth, but the mouth of the wise man is in his heart."

Benjamin Franklin (1706–1790)
U.S. writer, scientist, and politician

Superior vena cava delivers deoxygenated blood from the upper part of the body.

In the center of your chest, angled down and to the left and protected by your ribs, lies your body's motor—the heart. It is a small organ, but every day it ceaselessly pumps blood through the 62,000-mi. (100,000-km) network of blood vessels that reaches all over the human body. Without the nutrients and oxygen that this blood supplies to your tissues and organs, your body would not be able to function.

AORTA—*the main artery that carries blood from the heart all over the body*

How the heart works

The heart is made up of a special type of muscle—cardiac muscle. This pumps the blood through four hollow chambers, which each have one-way valves between them that keep the blood flowing in the right direction. The upper chambers are called atria and the lower chambers are called ventricles.

A person's heart is around the same size as his or her clenched fist.

Pulmonary veins carry oxygenated (oxygen-rich) blood back to the heart.

Right atrium pushes deoxygenated blood from the body into the right ventricle.

The heart muscle

Unlike the body's other muscles, cardiac muscle exists only in the heart. It is very strong and contracts and relaxes automatically. These actions are controlled by cells called pacemaker cells, which regulate the rate at which the heart beats.

chordae tendineae, known as the heartstrings

Right ventricle pumps blood into the pulmonary arteries and to the lungs.

The heartstrings

The chordae tendineae, or heartstrings, are cordlike tendons. They connect the pulmonary valve to the muscles in the right ventricle and the aortic valve to the muscles of the left ventricle. They help pull the valves open and also prevent them from turning inside out.

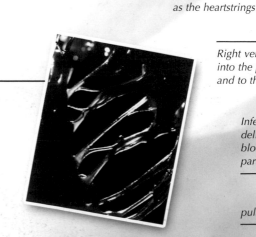

Inferior vena cava delivers deoxygenated blood from the lower part of the body.

pulmonary valve

> In an average person, the heart beats around 100,000 times per day and around three billion times in a lifetime.

left-hand side of the body

Deoxygenated blood is pulled from the body by the right side of the heart and pumped to the lungs.

Oxygenated blood from the lungs is pulled into the left side of the heart and pumped out around the body.

Aorta carries oxygenated blood from the heart around the body.

Pulmonary artery carries blood to the lungs to collect oxygen.

pulmonary veins from the lungs

Left atrium pushes oxygenated blood from the lungs into the left ventricle.

aortic valve

Blood flow in the heart

Heart muscle has its own blood supply—the coronary arteries (shown in white). If these become blocked, the connecting vessels between the arteries can sometimes provide an alternative route for the flow of blood.

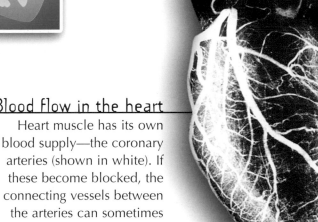

⊖ HEARTBEATS AND THEIR CYCLE

The heart contracts and relaxes around 70 times per minute. With each heartbeat, the four chambers inside the heart are filled with more blood. The rate at which the heart beats is managed by the nervous system. When you exercise or are upset or excited, your heart beats quicker to carry more oxygen to your muscles.

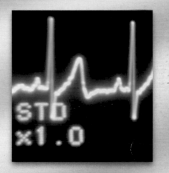

an ECG (electrocardiogram) of a normal heartbeat

Left ventricle pumps oxygenated blood into the aorta and around the body.

myocardium— the muscular wall of the heart

Septum—a wall of muscle—separates the two atria and the two ventricles.

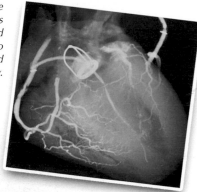

Artificial valves

Occasionally, parts of the heart do not work very well or may fail completely. This x-ray shows a mechanical heart valve (top right) that has replaced the aortic valve between the left ventricle and the aorta. It has taken over the job of controlling the flow of blood into the aorta.

LUNGS AND BREATHING

Your body needs oxygen, and you get this from the air that you breathe. Air enters and leaves your body through the respiratory system. It first passes from your nose and mouth into the trachea, or windpipe. This divides into two tubes called bronchi that lead into the lungs. Inside the lungs, a process called gas exchange takes place. This is when oxygen from the air passes into the blood system and carbon dioxide passes out as a waste product. Exhaling (breathing out) removes the carbon dioxide from the body.

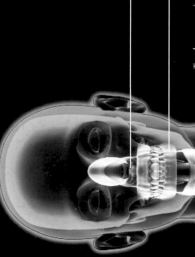

"A large nose is the mark of a witty, courteous, affable, generous, and liberal man."

Cyrano de Bergerac (1619–1655)
French duelist and writer

nostrils

mouth

Trachea, or windpipe, has a flap of skin at the top to prevent food from entering.

larynx, or voice box

lungs protected by the rib cage

Bronchi branch out from the trachea and then divide into bronchioles.

diaphragm—a dome-shaped muscle separating the lungs from the stomach

How the respiratory system works

Your nose, throat, larynx (voice box), trachea (windpipe), and lungs all make up the respiratory system. When you inhale (breathe in), you pull in air through your nostrils and mouth. By doing this, you fill the lungs with oxygen-rich air. This oxygen, vital to the body's well-being, is transferred to the blood. The blood then carries the oxygen to every part of the body, feeding its tissues and organs.

The trachea

The bony tube of the trachea is made out of rings of cartilage that help keep your airways open. The trachea has mucus-secreting glands such as the one at the center of this picture. These add moisture to the air as it passes through.

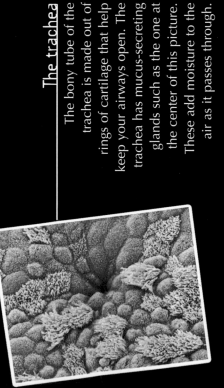

> **LUNG**—*one of two elastic organs that pull fresh air into the body and expel stale air from it*

Inhaling and exhaling

When you inhale, the diaphragm moves down and the muscles between your ribs pull outward. This sucks air in through your airways and inflates your lungs. When you exhale, the diaphragm moves up and the muscles relax. This pushes the air back out, deflating your lungs.

Cleaning and clearing

In the nose and trachea, tiny hairs called cilia filter out dust and other particles. The cilia move back and forth with the passage of air. They sweep the foreign matter in a flow of mucus back out of the nose or mouth or down into the intestines.

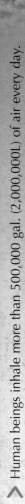

Bronchi and bronchioles

Inside the lungs, the bronchi branch into smaller tubes called bronchioles. These end in alveoli, where gas exchange takes place. The alveoli are only one cell thick and are surrounded by tiny blood vessels called capillaries. These are lined with a thin layer of cells, through which the gases easily pass in and out.

Each lung contains up to 400 million tiny alveoli.

The network of bronchi, bronchioles, and alveoli is called the bronchial tree.

alveolus lined with a single layer of cells

Sac shape provides a large surface area for gas exchange.

● SPEECH

When air is passed out of the lungs, it vibrates over the vocal cords in the larynx and passes out through the mouth and nose. You can shape this vibration into words and other sounds. You do this by controlling the muscles that widen or narrow the larynx and by using your tongue, teeth, and lips to create different effects.

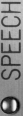

❯ Human beings inhale more than 500,000 gal. (2,000,000L) of air every day.

Nervous tissue is made up of two cell types—neurons, such as the one below, and glial cells. Neurons transmit nerve messages. Nourishing glial cells surround neurons.

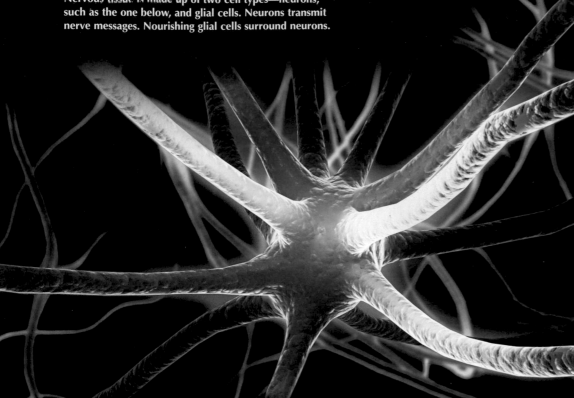

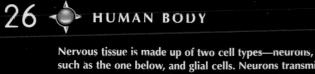

⊖ REFLEXES

The spinal cord controls involuntary and rapid actions that are called reflexes. These include closing your eyes because the light is too bright or pulling your hand away from the heat of a flame. The signals do not travel up to the brain for a decision to be made, so the actions happen automatically and very quickly. Digestion and blood pressure are both regulated by reflexes known as autonomic reflexes.

Racing motorcyclists have high-speed reflexes.

NERVES AND REFLEXES

Neurons, or nerve cells, carry messages all over the body. There are three types—sensory neurons, interneurons, and motor neurons. Sensory neurons are stimulated by touch, taste, smell, sound, and sight. Interneurons exist in the brain and spinal cord and are stimulated by sensory neurons or other interneurons. Motor neurons, stimulated by sensory neurons and interneurons, transmit signals from the central nervous system to muscles and glands that carry out actions.

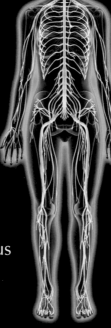

"I have bad reflexes. I was once run over by a car being pushed by two guys."

Woody Allen (born 1935)
U.S. writer, comedian, actor, and movie director

Nervous system
This huge network of neurons transmits messages all over the human body via nerve impulses. The brain and the spinal cord form the central nervous system. This works without stopping, collecting information and sending out messages that result in bodily activity.

∨ NERVE—a bundle of fibers that transmits impulses

> There are almost 47 mi. (75km) of nerves running through the human body.

Axons, the main nerve fibers of a neuron, carry nerve impulses. Axons connecting the spinal cord to the feet can be as long as 3 ft. (1m).

A protective coating called the myelin sheath wraps around the axon, insulating the nerve and helping impulses travel.

Neurons

Each neuron has a cell body with short "feelers" called dendrites. These pick up nerve impulses from nearby neurons. A long nerve fiber, the axon, then carries the impulses away to be picked up by the dendrites of other neurons. This picture shows a cut-through view of neurons.

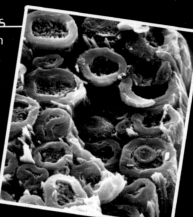

http://faculty.washington.edu/chudler/cells.html

Nerve impulses

When they are stimulated, neurons undergo chemical changes. These produce waves of electricity—nerve impulses—that travel down the axon of the nerve to its junction with another nerve or cell. Nerve signals may be excitatory—stimulating the cells that they connect to—or inhibitory—turning down the activity of the next cell or making it less sensitive to stimulation by other nerves.

dendrite—a "feeler" connected to the main cell body

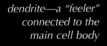

At synapses, the nerve impulses are converted into a chemical message.

The chemicals are released and cross the gap at the synapse to attach to receptors on the next cell—and pass the message on.

receptor

soma, or cell body

Synapses

In this magnified image, two branching nerve fibers (purple) can be seen connecting to the surface of a neuron. The junctions where they touch are called synapses. Impulses run down the fibers and into the neuron, and this stimulates the cell. Impulses cross from one neuron to another at synapses.

Gray and white matter

The tissue of the cerebrum has two layers. The outer gray layer is the cerebral cortex, known as gray matter. The inner layer, or white matter, is mostly made up of nerve fibers. These fibers send information all over the brain.

gray matter

white matter

Left hemisphere (half) of the cerebrum controls the right side of the body; the right hemisphere controls the left side of the body.

Cerebellum ("little brain") controls balance, limb movement, and coordination.

Brain stem connects the brain to the spinal column.

BRAIN AND SPINAL CORD

An incredible organ—your brain—is at the center of a nervous system that controls everything, from thinking to blinking. The brain is very fragile, but it is protected by three membranes, known as the meninges, and the hard bone of the skull. The bundle of nerve fibers that make up the spinal cord reaches from the brain right down along the length of the back. It carries messages between the brain and the nerves in the rest of the body.

"It is the brain, the little gray cells, on which one must rely."

Hercule Poirot
*fictional Belgian detective created by
mystery writer Agatha Christie (1890–1976)*

How the brain works

When someone reads, the sensory information is passed from the eyes to the largest part of the brain, the cerebrum. This is used for thinking, reasoning, and memorizing. It also controls muscle movements. If it is a funny book, the brain transmits that information via the nervous system, and the person exercises those muscles that cause them to laugh.

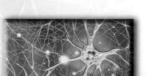

> **GRAY MATTER**—*the surface layer of the cerebrum and the inner part of the spinal cord*

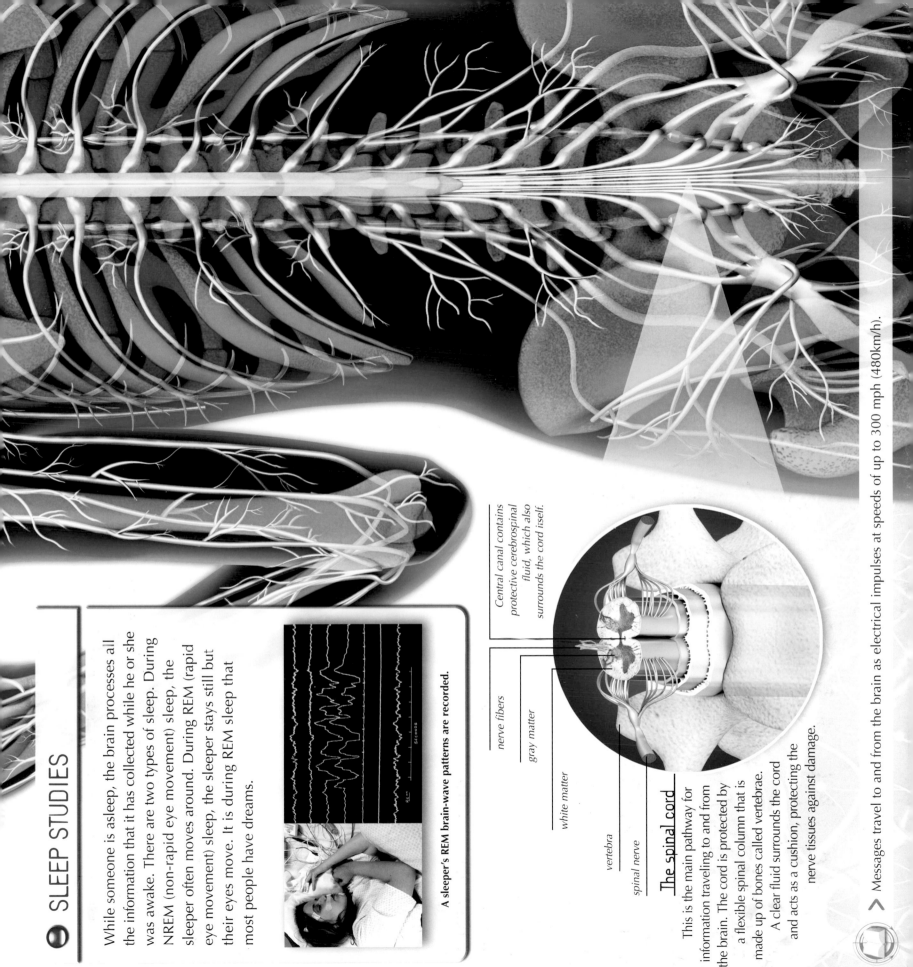

SLEEP STUDIES

While someone is asleep, the brain processes all the information that it has collected while he or she was awake. There are two types of sleep. During NREM (non-rapid eye movement) sleep, the sleeper often moves around. During REM (rapid eye movement) sleep, the sleeper stays still but their eyes move. It is during REM sleep that most people have dreams.

A sleeper's REM brain-wave patterns are recorded.

Central canal contains protective cerebrospinal fluid, which also surrounds the cord itself.

nerve fibers

gray matter

white matter

vertebra

spinal nerve

The spinal cord

This is the main pathway for information traveling to and from the brain. The cord is protected by a flexible spinal column that is made up of bones called vertebrae. A clear fluid surrounds the cord and acts as a cushion, protecting the nerve tissues against damage.

> Messages travel to and from the brain as electrical impulses at speeds of up to 300 mph (480km/h).

http://kidshealth.org/kid/htbw/brain.html

TOUCH, TASTE, AND SMELL

SALIVA—a fluid that is released by the salivary glands into the mouth in order to moisten food

Unlike other senses, the sense of touch is found all over the body—mostly wherever there is skin. Touch allows us to identify different types of pressure, as well as temperature and pain. Taste and smell are more specialized senses that can detect chemical substances. These senses function mostly in one place—in the mouth for taste and in the nose for smell—and react to specific stimuli.

Reacting to pain

Nerve endings in the skin's dermis enable us to sense pressure, different temperatures, and pain. If you burn your hand while you are cooking, signals from the nerves speed through the central nervous system, ensuring that you move your hand away from the source of heat—immediately.

Invisible scent molecules in the air stimulate nerve cells to tell the brain what type of odor they have.

"All of life is a dispute over taste and tasting."

Friedrich Nietzsche (1844–1900)
German philosopher

⊖ "SENSING" FOOD

Our sense of taste and our enjoyment of food are heavily dependent on two other senses—smell and touch. Taste buds in the mouth and nerves in the nose gather information and communicate it to the brain. Nerve endings in the lips and mouth tell us whether the food or drink is hot or cold and what texture it has.

A chef tastes and smells his food.

> The highest recorded speed of a sneeze is 102 mph (165km/h).

http://faculty.washington.edu/chudler/chsense.html

Picking up the scent

Sniffing brings air into the nasal cavity, where tiny cilia filter out dust and bacteria. The air, containing scent molecules, passes through a thick layer of mucus to wash over the olfactory nerve endings. The scent molecules stimulate the nerve endings, which then send signals to the olfactory bulb.

The microscopic, hairlike cilia are covered in a sticky mucus, which traps dust and other particles.

sinus—a space within the skull bones—connects with nasal cavity

olfactory bulb—carries nerve impulses from receptors to brain

Smell receptors in the olfactory nerves can distinguish between 10,000 different odors.

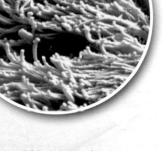

Olfactory hairs

Tiny nerve projections called olfactory hairs stick out into the nasal cavity. They detect chemicals that enter the nasal passage. Olfactory cells, which cover the roof of the nasal cavity, send the information to the brain.

Air enters the nasal cavity through the nostrils.

nasal cavity

jawbone

There are around 10,000 taste buds on the tongue, the roof and back of the mouth, and in the larynx.

Nerves collect sensory impulses from all parts of the tongue.

Spiky papillae on the surface help the tongue grip.

taste pore with taste bud underneath

Taste buds

Receptor cells inside the taste buds in your mouth detect chemicals in the food that is dissolved in saliva. They send messages to your brain via sensory nerves. The brain then tells you what flavors you are tasting when you eat and drink.

larynx

CORNEA—the transparent (clear) tissue at the front of the eye that lets in light

SIGHT AND SOUND

Sight and hearing are the senses that provide your brain with the most information about the world. Set in a protective bony socket, the eye converts light into nerve impulses. It sends these to the brain, which interprets and reacts to them. Sound waves travel through the outer ear and cause vibrations in the middle ear. The vibrations are converted into nerve impulses in the inner ear. These impulses are also sent to the brain.

auricle, or pinna

Ear canal produces earwax to clean and lubricate.

⊖ BALANCE

Your ears also help you balance and stay upright. Inside the inner ear, the three semicircular canals and two sacs, called the utricle and saccule, continually send nerve signals to the brain about your body's movement and posture.

A skateboarder slides along a railing.

Seeing is believing

When you look at something, the light reflected from the object passes through the cornea and iris and into the pupil of your eye. The pupil is a lens that projects what you are seeing onto the back of the eye. From there, the optic nerve carries the signal to the brain.

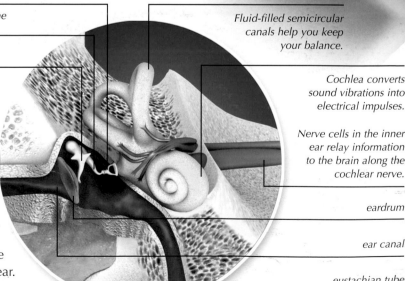

stapes, or stirrup bone

incus, or anvil bone

malleus, or hammer bone

Fluid-filled semicircular canals help you keep your balance.

Cochlea converts sound vibrations into electrical impulses.

Nerve cells in the inner ear relay information to the brain along the cochlear nerve.

The middle ear and inner ear

In the middle ear, sound hits the eardrum, causing it to vibrate. These vibrations pass to the body's three smallest bones—the malleus, the incus, and the stapes. These transfer the vibrations into the inner ear.

eardrum

ear canal

eustachian tube

 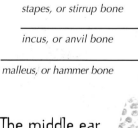 > The human eye can see up to ten million different colors.

Lachrymal gland produces tears to moisten and protect the eye.

Eye contains a clear jelly called the vitreous body.

Protecting the eyes

Eyelids and eyelashes protect your eyes from dust, dirt, and bright light. Every time you blink, your eyelids spread tears over your eyes. These tears wash away anything that irritates your eyes.

blind spot on retina, where optic nerve leaves the eyeball

Optic nerve carries messages to the brain.

Tough, white sclera protects the eyeball.

Structure of the eye

The cornea allows light into the eye. The iris changes the size of the pupil at its center to control the amount of light that it lets in. The cornea helps the lens focus rays onto the retina, a light-sensitive membrane at the back of the eye.

Transparent, dome-shaped cornea lets through light.

Pupil channels light into the eye.

Iris gives the eye its color.

Lens alters its shape to focus the light.

Retina contains light-sensitive "rod" and "cone" cells.

Rods and cones

There are two types of light-sensing cells in the retina: rods and cones. The 120 million rods are sensitive, even in low light. There are around seven million cones, and in bright light they provide color vision.

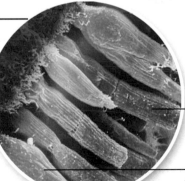

rod (blue)

cone (green)

The image formed on the retina is upside down, but the brain interprets this so that it is "seen" as being upright.

An upside-down image of the object focuses on the retina.

The object reflects light.

Nearsightedness and farsightedness

If light rays are not bent enough by the cornea and lens, they focus behind the retina. This makes close objects appear blurred (farsightedness). If light rays are bent too much, they focus in front of the retina. This makes distant objects appear blurred (nearsightedness).

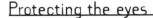
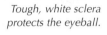

GLANDS AND HORMONES

The endocrine system is made up of glands, or groups of cells, that are scattered throughout the body. These glands release more than 20 chemical messengers called hormones into the bloodstream to reach distant parts of the body. There, the hormones bind with specialized hormone receptors. This action triggers responses in different bodily functions such as metabolism, growth, and sexual development.

thyroid gland—controls rate of metabolism

parathyroid glands—help control calcium levels

kidney (see pages 40–41)

adrenal gland—functions include maintaining blood pressure

ovaries—produce female sex hormones and eggs for reproduction

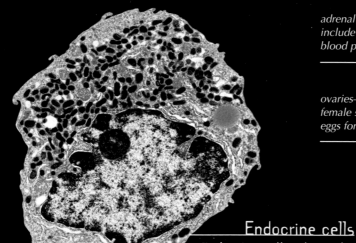

colored micrograph image of an endocrine cell

Endocrine cells

Endocrine cells release the hormones that travel through the bloodstream to target cells in the body. Some hormones are linked with specific jobs. Somatotropin is secreted by cells in the pituitary gland to stimulate growth, and parathyroid glands release a hormone that controls the amount of calcium in the blood.

Female glands

The glands that are the same in both females and males are the hypothalamus, pituitary, pineal, thyroid, parathyroid, thymus, adrenal, and pancreas. Two female sex hormones, estrogen and progesterone, are produced in the female reproductive glands, the ovaries.

> Laughing lowers the levels of stress hormones and strengthens the immune system.

Glands in the brain

Nerve cells in the hypothalamus stimulate or limit hormone production by the pituitary gland. The pituitary gland is only the size of a pea, but it is often called the "master gland" because it produces hormones that control other glands.

pineal gland—secretes a hormone that helps control sleep patterns

thalamus

hypothalamus—the main link between the endocrine system and nervous system

pituitary gland

pancreas—secretes hormones to control blood sugar and glucose metabolism

testes—produce male sex hormones and sperm for reproduction

Male glands

These glands also include the hypothalamus, pituitary, pineal, thyroid, parathyroid, thymus, adrenal, and pancreas. The male sex hormones are called androgens. The main androgen is testosterone, which is produced in the male reproductive glands, the testes.

⊝ EPINEPHRINE

crystals of epinephrine

Epinephrine, or adrenaline, is produced in the adrenal glands above each kidney. When someone is stressed, large amounts of this hormone pass into the bloodstream. This widens the airways of the lungs and releases sugar that is stored in the liver. These things enable the muscles to work harder.

Anger and fear are two powerful emotions that cause epinephrine to be released into the bloodstream.

DIGESTION

Food and drinks need to be broken down so that the body can absorb nutrients into the blood. This is handled by the digestive system. It begins in the mouth, where you chew and swallow. The food passes into the esophagus, which leads into the stomach. There, it is churned up, and digestive juices help break down the food. The stomach contents are gradually emptied into the small intestine, where nutrients are absorbed, before being further processed in the large intestine.

"Happiness: a good bank account, a good cook, and a good digestion."

Jean Jacques Rousseau (1712–1778)
French philosopher

The digestive system

The digestive system is made up of a series of organs that are connected by a long tube that stretches from the mouth to the anus. The organs, which include the stomach, pancreas, liver, and intestines, help digest the food as it travels through the system.

A BALANCED DIET

In order to be healthy, we need a balance of the following: carbohydrates for energy; protein for growth and repair, and fat for energy. We also require vitamins (A, the B group, C, D, and E), as well as mineral salts: calcium for bones, teeth, muscles, and nerves; iron to make hemoglobin in the blood; iodine to make hormones that control our metabolism; and sodium, potassium, and chlorine for the muscles and nerves. We also need fiber to make the bowels work properly.

There are five main food groups: grains (bread, cereal, and pasta); fruit and vegetables; meat, fish, beans, and nuts; milk and dairy foods; and fat and sugar.

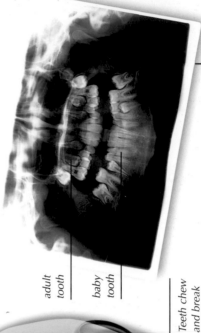

adult tooth

baby tooth

Teeth and saliva

As your teeth cut up and chew the food that you eat, salivary glands produce saliva. This watery substance moistens food so that you can swallow it easily. Our baby teeth, or "milk teeth"—around 20 in number—are gradually replaced by 32 adult teeth as we grow up.

Teeth chew and break up food for swallowing.

Muscles in esophagus push food into stomach.

> **DIGESTION**—*the process by which food is broken down and absorbed into the bloodstream*

Villi

Sprouting from the wall of the small intestine are small, hairlike projections called villi. These greatly increase the wall's surface area so that more food particles can be captured. The blood inside the villi absorbs the nutrients.

Bacteria in the ileum

Here, bacteria (yellow-green) and tiny pieces of food (blue) are on the villi of the ileum, a part of the small intestine. Bacteria in the intestines help break down the food to provide more nutrients.

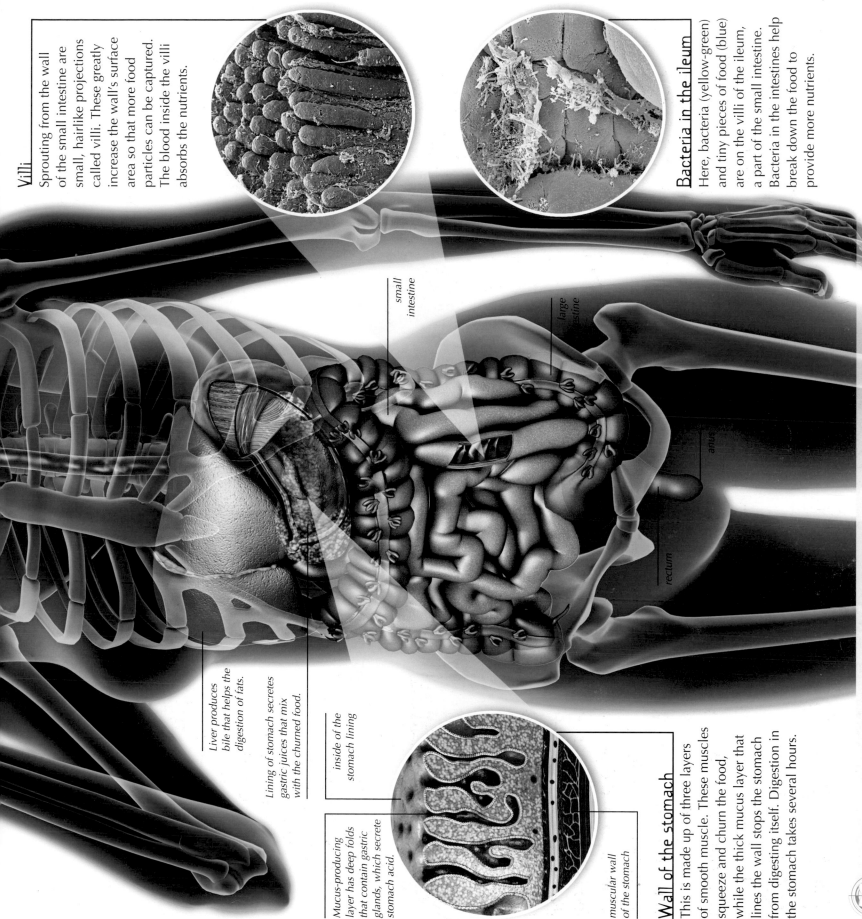

small intestine

large intestine

anus

rectum

Liver produces bile that helps the digestion of fats.

Lining of stomach secretes gastric juices that mix with the churned food.

inside of the stomach lining

Mucus-producing layer has deep folds that contain gastric glands, which secrete stomach acid.

muscular wall of the stomach

Wall of the stomach

This is made up of three layers of smooth muscle. These muscles squeeze and churn the food, while the thick mucus layer that lines the wall stops the stomach from digesting itself. Digestion in the stomach takes several hours.

> Your small intestine is amazingly long—up to 23 ft. (7m) in length.

http://yucky.discovery.com/flash/body/pg000126.html

PROCESSING AND CLEANING

After food has been processed by the stomach and has arrived in the small intestine, two more organs continue the process of digestion. The pancreas produces a juice containing enzymes, which cause chemical reactions that break down the fat, carbohydrates, and protein in the food. The liver produces a digestive juice called bile, which dissolves fats so that they can be absorbed. The remaining waste then passes into the large intestine.

How the system works

Undigested food and water travel into the large intestine through a one-way valve. Inside the large intestine, water is removed from the food so that only solid matter is left. This matter then travels to the rectum, where it is stored until it can be expelled through the anus.

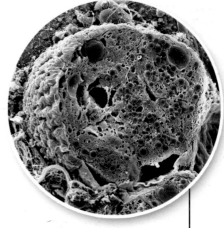

Cells in the pancreas

Pancreatic cells, such as the one above, produce digestive enzymes that pass into the small intestine. There, they break down carbohydrates, fats, and proteins.

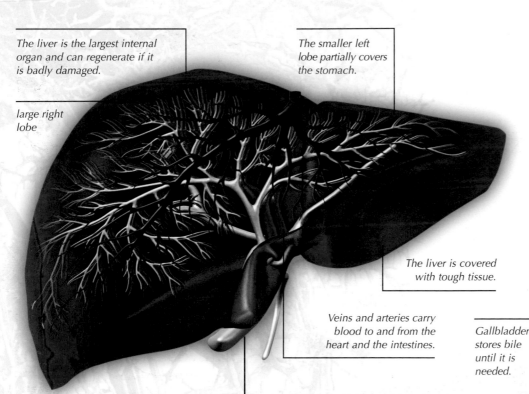

The liver is the largest internal organ and can regenerate if it is badly damaged.

The smaller left lobe partially covers the stomach.

large right lobe

The liver is covered with tough tissue.

Veins and arteries carry blood to and from the heart and the intestines.

Gallblader stores bile until it is needed.

bile ducts

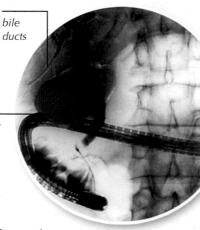

Inside the liver

The liver has tiny chemical processing plants, called lobules, that contain cells called hepatocytes. These cells form 80 percent of the liver and process the blood that is pumped through them. They store some parts of the blood, clean others, and release those, such as blood sugar (glucose), that the body needs.

Bile and its storage

Bile produced by the liver is carried through the bile ducts (top left) to the small intestine, where it helps digest fat.

 > The large intestine is twice as wide as the small intestine but only one quarter of its length.

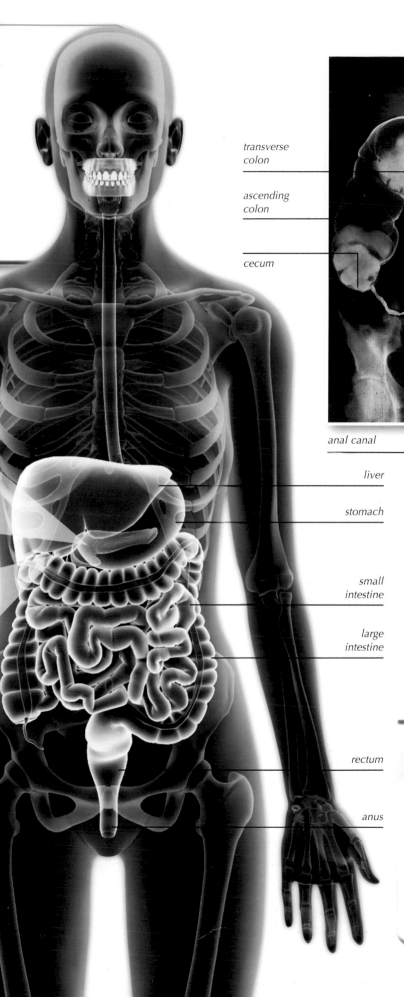

transverse colon

ascending colon

cecum

liver

stomach

small intestine

large intestine

rectum

anus

anal canal

The large intestine

The large intestine is connected to the small intestine at one end and to the anus at the other. This x-ray picture was created by passing a liquid containing a metal, barium, through the intestine. X-rays do not pass through barium, so the large intestine shows up much clearer.

descending colon

S-shaped sigmoid colon

rectum

www.bbc.co.uk/science/humanbody/body/factfiles/liver/liver.shtml

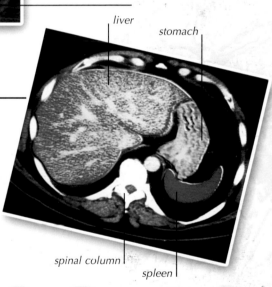

liver

stomach

spinal column

spleen

The spleen

The spleen contains white blood cells that help fight infections. It also destroys old red blood cells and cleans the blood. This scan shows the spleen in a slice through the body, looking upward from the feet.

⊖ THE APPENDIX

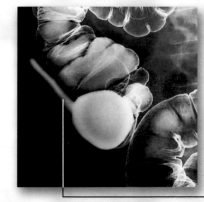

The appendix is a narrow tube that projects (sticks out) from the rounded cecum (center left) at one end of the large intestine. It is around 4 in. (10cm) long in the average adult and can be straight (left) or curled. Its exact function is unknown.

appendix

WASTE MANAGEMENT

The kidneys and bladder control the balance of the water and salts in the blood. They also control what is removed from the blood as waste products. Most of the fluid that passes through the kidneys is cleaned and returned to the bloodstream. The rest is passed through to the bladder to be expelled from the body through the process of urination.

adrenal gland

A protective renal capsule surrounds each kidney.

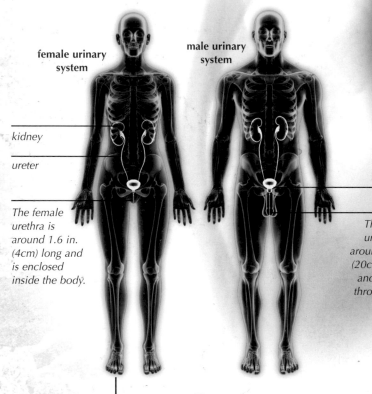

female urinary system

male urinary system

kidney

ureter

bladder

The female urethra is around 1.6 in. (4cm) long and is enclosed inside the body.

The male urethra is around 8 in. (20cm) long and passes through the penis.

The urinary system

This system, which removes waste called urea from the blood, is made up of the organs, tubes, muscles, and nerves that create, store, and carry urine. These include two kidneys, two ureters, the bladder, two sphincter muscles, and the urethra.

How the kidneys work

Your two kidneys filter blood to remove waste products and excess water. These become urine, which flows into your bladder through two long tubes called ureters. The kidneys also produce important hormones that control blood pressure, maintain calcium for bones, and stimulate bone marrow to produce red blood cells.

> A kidney stone, measuring 7 in. (17.9cm) in length and weighing 4.2 lbs. (1.9kg), was removed from a 62-year-old Brazilian in August 2003.

Glomeruli and nephrons

Inside the kidneys are clusters of tiny blood vessels called glomeruli (right). These are surrounded by a double-walled container known as a Bowman's capsule. Each capsule and its tiny, urine-collecting tube are together called a nephron. The glomeruli filter blood and remove waste material.

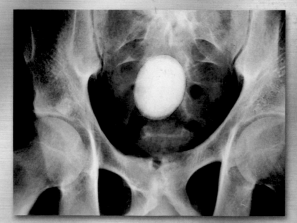

coiled glomerulus

blood vessel that supplies the glomeruli

false color image of glomeruli

www.innerbody.com/image/urinov.html

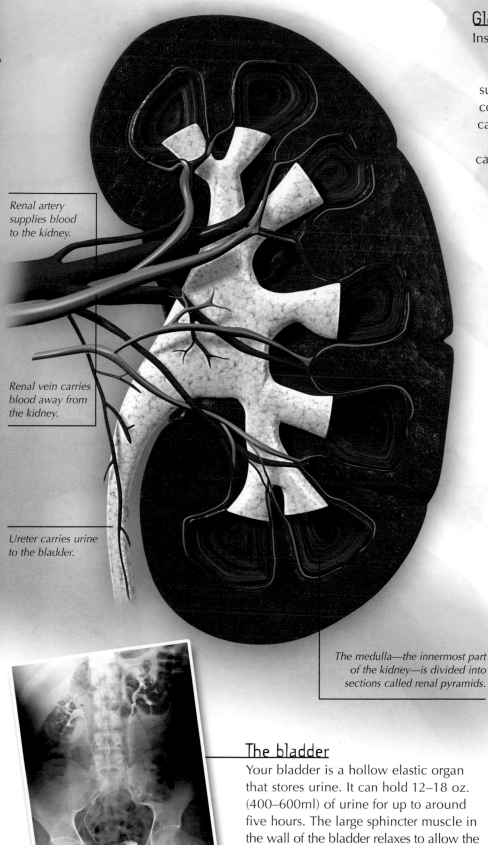

Renal artery supplies blood to the kidney.

Renal vein carries blood away from the kidney.

Ureter carries urine to the bladder.

The medulla—the innermost part of the kidney—is divided into sections called renal pyramids.

bladder

KIDNEY STONES

Tiny crystals often form in urine, but they pass through the system without difficulty. Sometimes, the waste products in the bladder crystallize, forming hard "stones" that are usually made up of calcium. Most stones are relatively small—around 0.08–0.8 in. (0.2–2cm) across—but sometimes large ones form and have to be surgically removed.

x-ray of a large stone, formed in the bladder of a 65-year-old man

The bladder

Your bladder is a hollow elastic organ that stores urine. It can hold 12–18 oz. (400–600ml) of urine for up to around five hours. The large sphincter muscle in the wall of the bladder relaxes to allow the bladder to fill up. When you go to the bathroom, it contracts and squeezes out urine through a tube called the urethra.

NEW LIFE

FETUS—an unborn child from the eighth week of its development in the womb

In humans, sex cells called sperm are produced by the male. These are put into the female when a male penis is inserted into the female vagina. A single sperm fertilizes (joins with) an egg that is produced by the female, and the egg then embeds itself in the wall of her uterus. The first eight weeks of development are known as the embryo stage, during which the egg divides and multiplies until it is a tiny human. After that, the developing baby is called a fetus.

Millions of sperm are released, but only a few reach the uterus and fallopian tubes.

Head of sperm contains genetic material in the center, in its nucleus.

Ovum nucleus also contains genetic material.

Fertilization

Fertilization is the process by which the genetic material of the sperm and the ovum (egg) merge together to form new life. Only one sperm will get through the surface of the ovum to fertilize it. Instantly, a membrane forms around the ovum, and no other sperm can enter.

Male reproductive system

The male testes produce sperm and the sex hormone testosterone. The sperm are pushed out in a nourishing fluid, called semen, up the urethra, and out through the penis.

Seminal vesicle produces most of the seminal fluid or semen.

Prostate gland produces some seminal fluid.

Vas deferens is a muscular tube that pushes sperm through.

Female reproductive system

Unlike the male sex organs, the female ovaries, fallopian tubes, and uterus are all inside the body. They produce ova, or eggs, and nourish and protect any babies that may result.

Uterus, or womb, protects and nourishes the baby before it is born.

Ovary produces a ripe egg at regular monthly intervals.

Breasts produce milk after childbirth.

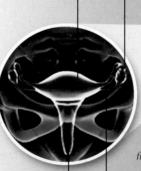

Fallopian tube carries ripe egg from the ovary to the uterus.

Urethra carries sperm from the testes or urine from the bladder.

The vagina is where sperm enters. It becomes the birth canal when a baby is born.

Testes are situated outside the body.

 > The fetus has a covering of fine, dark hair during the fourth and fifth months of pregnancy.

Fetal development

Pregnancy lasts for around 40 weeks. By the tenth week, the fetus is around 1.2 in. (3cm) long and weighs less than 0.14 oz. (4g). However, all the vital organs are already formed, and the fetus can swallow and kick. By the 35th week, the lungs, digestive system, and hearing are all fully developed.

The amniotic sac contains around 0.2 gal. (1L) of fluid.

Umbilical cord connects the fetus to the placenta.

This baby is around 19.5 in. (50cm) long and weighs approximately 7.7 lbs. (3.5kg). It is full term and ready to be born.

The placenta is an organ that develops inside the uterus during early pregnancy, supplying the fetus with oxygen and nutrients, while removing any waste products

head of baby "engaged" in opening of the uterus

The cervix opens up into the vagina, or birth canal.

http://kidshealth.org/parent/general/body_basics/male_reproductive.html

⊖ GROWTH AND AGING

People develop both physically and mentally throughout their lives. Babies and small children depend on their parents, but as they grow, they become independent, passing through puberty to become adults. In later life, signs of aging often include physical and mental changes, but many older people remain fully active and healthy.

four generations of the same family

GLOSSARY

antibody
A substance released by the immune system to destroy microorganisms that cause diseases.

bacteria
A group of microorganisms, some of which cause diseases.

base
One of four substances—adenine, cytosine, guanine, and thymine—that combine to give genetic instructions in molecules of DNA.

blood pressure
The force of blood pushing against the walls of the main arteries.

bone marrow
Soft tissue found inside bones, some of which produces new blood cells.

carbohydrate
One of the main components of food that is broken down in the body to provide energy, partly in the form of glucose.

cartilage
Tough, flexible tissue that covers the surface of bones at the joints and protects against any damage.

CAT scan
Computerized axial tomography—a type of x-ray that provides cross-sectional ("sliced") views of the body.

cell
The basic unit of all living things. A cell is able to reproduce itself exactly.

chromosome
One of 46 threadlike structures in the nucleus of a cell that carries genetic information in the form of genes.

cilium (*cilia*, plural)
A short, hairlike projection that sweeps backward and forward. Cells use cilia to move things across their surface.

dermis
The thick layer of skin that lies beneath the outer layer, the epidermis.

DNA
Deoxyribonucleic acid—the genetic material of living organisms that carries the coded instructions needed for them to develop and reproduce.

ECG
Electrocardiogram—a technique for recording the electrical activity of the heart.

enzyme
A protein that acts as a catalyst— a substance that helps speed up the rate of chemical reactions in the body.

epidermis
The outer layer of the skin.

feces
The solid waste of undigested food that is expelled from the body through the anus.

genetics
The science of inheritance and how genes are passed on from one generation of living things to the next.

gland
A group of cells or an organ that produces substances, including hormones, that are needed by the body.

hormone
A chemical messenger that is produced and released by an endocrine gland.

keratin
A tough protein that is found in hair, nails, and the upper layer of the epidermis.

lymph
A fluid that flows from the tissues to the blood as part of the lymphatic system.

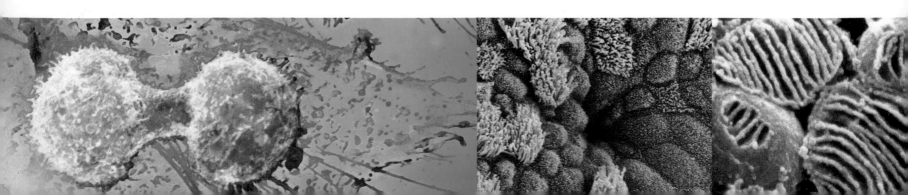

melanin

A dark brown or black pigment that gives color to skin, hair, and the iris of the eye.

membrane

A thin layer of tissue that surrounds organs or lines the body surface, both internally and externally.

metabolism

All the chemical and physical changes that take place in the body and enable it to grow and function.

molecule

A chemical unit that consists of two or more atoms.

MRI

Magnetic resonance imaging—a technique that uses high-frequency radio waves to produce electronic images, or scans, of the body.

mucous membrane

The layer that lines body cavities, such as the nasal passages, and that secretes mucus.

mucus

Thick, slimy fluid secreted by mucous membranes to moisten and lubricate.

neuron

One of the nerve cells that carries electrical signals through the nervous system.

nucleus

The center of a cell.

nutrient

A substance, such as a carbohydrate, vitamin, or protein, needed for the body to grow and function properly.

organ

A part of the body, composed of more than one tissue, that is responsible for a particular function. The heart, liver, and lungs are examples of organs.

perspiration

A salty fluid secreted by the sweat glands of the skin.

plasma

The liquid part of the blood that makes up around 50 percent of it.

platelet

A disk-shaped cell in the blood. Platelets are important for blood clotting.

pore

A small opening on the skin's surface.

protein

A molecule that supplies essential amino acids to the body and that forms the basis of other substances such as keratin, enzymes, and antibodies.

puberty

A period during adolescence when the body's reproductive system starts working and the body changes from a child's to an adult's.

reflex

An automatic and immediate response that helps protect the body.

REM

Rapid eye movement—the stage of sleep during which the muscles of the eyeballs are constantly moving.

replication

The process by which DNA makes exact copies of itself when a cell divides.

saliva

A fluid released by the salivary glands to keep the mouth moist.

vitamin

One of a group of substances in food that are needed in very small amounts for healthy growth.

INDEX

INVESTIGATE

Find out what the experts know about the human body and how it works and explore it yourself by checking out books, websites, museums, and art galleries.

Museums and exhibitions

Many museums have interactive displays about the human body, and you can learn a lot by visiting their special exhibitions.

 Body by Robert Winston (Dorling Kindersley)

 Human Body Gallery, Science Museum of Minnesota, St. Paul, MN 55102

www.sciencemuseum.org.uk/WhoAmI/FindOutMore.aspx

main entrance to the Natural History Museum, London, England

Actors examine a corpse during filming for the TV show *CSI: Crime Scene Investigation*—a forensic science drama.

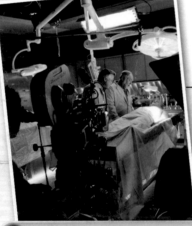

Television and media

Look out for television shows and articles in newspapers and magazines that feature different aspects of the human body and mind.

 Smithsonian magazine (monthly science publication)

 Inside the Living Body (National Geographic DVD)

www.bbc.co.uk/science/humanbody/

anatomical studies by Italian artist, inventor, and scientist Leonardo da Vinci (1452–1519)

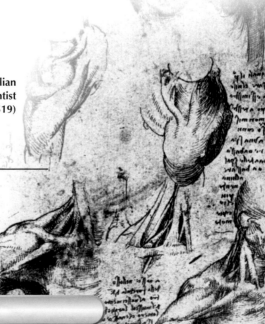

Art and history

Discover the human body in art galleries and books and find out how artists throughout the ages have drawn and painted people and their anatomy.

 Leonardo da Vinci and the Renaissance by Andrew Langley (Running Press Kids)

 The Metropolitan Museum of Art, New York, New York 10028

http://kids.tate.org.uk/games/art-detective/